ACCEPTABILITY
as a
FACTOR IN ARBITRATION
under an
EXISTING AGREEMENT

•

WILLIAM E. SIMKIN

•

Published for the
LABOR RELATIONS COUNCIL
of the
WHARTON SCHOOL OF FINANCE AND COMMERCE
by the
UNIVERSITY OF PENNSYLVANIA PRESS
Philadelphia
1952

Manufactured in the United States of America

William E. Simkin is a labor arbitrator who has served as a permanent arbitrator under a number of labor agreements and as ad hoc arbitrator. His full-time activities in this work have extended over a period of twelve years. He also served in several capacities for the National War Labor Board, including the Chairmanship of the Shipbuilding Commission. He was formerly President of the National Academy of Arbitrators.

CONTENTS

PREFACE

William E. Simkin has probably had a more varied and extensive experience as an arbitrator of grievances than any other person in the country. His distinguished standing in the field is attested by his selection in 1950 as president of the National Academy of Arbitrators. His considered views about the necessary principles and practices underlying the development of effective labor arbitration will, therefore, attract the attention of those interested in the problems of industrial relations. These views are cogently expressed in the monograph entitled *Acceptability as a Factor in Arbitration under an Existing Agreement.*

The study is notable for the author's careful weaving together of fundamental theory and down-to-earth practice. Grievance arbitration is quite logically perceived as a voluntarily adopted substitute for the strike or lockout. It must be appraised by employer and employees as preferable to the use of economic power to be useful. Every now and then, one or the other party to a labor agreement raises the doubt about "whether it is better to take our chances on the results of work stoppages" to resolve grievances. Mutual acceptability is a basic need and not a mere theoretical consideration. Nor can mutual acceptability be achieved by unthinking doctrinaire use of some alleged standard principles and practices. Just as collective-bargaining procedures vary as between different situations, so do arbitration procedures. At the same time, as the Simkin study makes clear, a careful development of the arbitration process with a view to the acceptability criterion in each situation is essential to attaining the full values of arbitration. It is exceedingly important, in my opinion, to evaluate grievance arbitration in such terms if the problems arising in the field of arbitration are to be soundly dealt with.

In developing the arbitration process, it does not suffice

for the parties to agree upon arbitration "in principle." There are too many potential points of disagreement about "the practice." If these matters are not resolved through understanding between the parties, the entire process can be brought into disrepute. The importance of agreed-upon details of arbitration principles, procedures, and practice is emphasized by Mr. Simkin's concept of arbitration as an aspect of the grievance procedure through which mutually acceptable solutions to industrial relations problems are found.

One further phase of Mr. Simkin's analysis deserves particular mention. It is suggested that union and management representatives should devote as much care and attention in devising the arbitration clause as they do with every other vital clause of their agreement. It is a fact that, in altogether too many instances, the arbitration clause itself does not reflect a complete meeting of minds about the manner in which grievances are to be finally settled. Once there is a mutual understanding on this point, the parties have then provided the necessary basis for developing the arbitration process, with the coöperation of the arbitrator, so as to serve their needs in a positive manner. This is merely another way of stating a major point made by Mr. Simkin: that the risks of arbitration can be and should be minimized. That can be done in his opinion—an opinion which I share—when the parties perceive the need for emphasizing the "acceptability factor" and take effective steps to place that factor in the arbitration equation.

Those interested in labor arbitration will undoubtedly find a stimulating experience when they read William Simkin's study. It constitutes an extremely valuable contribution to arbitration literature.

George W. Taylor

Philadelphia
July 1952

ACCEPTABILITY AS A FACTOR IN ARBITRATION UNDER AN EXISTING AGREEMENT

INTRODUCTION

It is a fundamental characteristic of collective bargaining that somehow and sometime an answer must be found to each problem within the scope of the process, an answer which is acceptable to both parties. The term "acceptable" needs some clarification.

Many of the long-run interests of both parties to a collective-bargaining relationship are in the same general direction. This underlying mutual interest is such a strong factor that many problems can be worked out in a way that is truly and immediately satisfactory to both sides. Solutions are often reached by collective bargaining where both parties walk away from the bargaining table with inner feelings of great accomplishment. This is the optimum of acceptability.

But other situations arise where the short-run interests of the parties are divergent or appear to be divergent, or where there may be important differences in long-run objectives. One party accepts the results of a particular bargain with reluctance and even with bitterness. While this form of acceptable answer is most likely to result after a strike or lockout at the time of contract negotiation, the same general reaction may be obtained in the absence of the use of economic strength in the settlement of grievances. This is the other side of the acceptability coin.

In between these extremes lie solutions reached by collective bargaining which are acceptable to the parties in varying mixtures of satisfaction and reluctance.

It is not realistic to assume that a union or a company is completely unified within itself. For example, a seniority issue almost always ranges one group of employees against another group. Or a solution fully acceptable to operating management may be quite distasteful to financial management. Thus the mixtures of immediate satisfaction and reluctance are composed in many cases of varying reactions within as well as between what are commonly thought of as the opposing parties.

One of the healthy aspects of collective bargaining is that the sense of responsibility and integrity possessed by mature people, together with the passage of time, do much to mellow the acceptability of a collective-bargaining solution which was adopted initially without enthusiasm by one or more of the interested participants.

Awards issued by arbitrators at the final step of the grievance procedure fall somewhere within a range of acceptability quite comparable to that indicated above. Some are recognized by both parties as just, workable, and excellent solutions of difficult problems. Some are considered "not too bad." Others are accepted by the parties with bitterness and only because there was advance agreement to abide by the award. In a few instances, a company or union feels that an award is so bad that it violates its own advance commitment to accept the decision as final and binding.

Is the level of acceptability of arbitration awards as high as the level of acceptability of decisions reached by direct negotiation? There is no ready answer to that important question, and this paper will not attempt directly to supply an answer. The purpose of the paper is to explore possible ways and means of increasing the acceptability of the systems of grievance arbitration and the decisions issued under such systems.

A significant element of the acceptability concept in direct negotiation is the development by the parties of a willingness to modify or even abandon positions taken at early stages of discussion. The hammering out of a solution to most problems or controversies in collective bargaining requires liberal doses of willingness to modify or even willingness to lose under persuasion.

One popular concept of arbitration is that the disputes decided by an arbitrator are irreconcilable, that the arbitrator is a judge who imposes his decision as a substitute for collective bargaining, and that arbitration exists only because collective bargaining is inadequate to fulfill its complete function.

On the basis of some twelve full years as a labor arbitrator, I am convinced that this concept of arbitration is only a minor part of the picture, even though it is a valid one in some few instances. Arbitration is a semi-judicial process, but it is also an integral part of the system of collective bargaining, and it includes the same necessary elements of collective bargaining—the development of willingness to modify and willingness to lose in the minds of the parties. The only essential difference between direct negotiation and arbitration is that the area of persuasion is broadened to include the arbitrator. In the last analysis, the arbitrator and the system of arbitration are successful only if the persuasive factors in the three-way equation (the company, the union and the arbitrator) are more vital than the exercise of authority.

ESSENTIAL CHARACTERISTICS OF VOLUNTARY ARBITRATION UNDER EXISTING AGREEMENTS

Relationship Between Arbitration Under an Agreement and the No-Strike, No-Lockout Clause

Individuals and groups have a normal desire to make their own decisions. They object to outside interference. The will to self-government is strong. This is particularly the case in labor relations. Companies which once resisted interference by representatives of organized employees in what was considered company business and have since accepted collective bargaining often become adamant in the position that the company and union should settle their own affairs without the intervention of any outsiders. Employees, having found new strength and power in organization, are generally equally reluctant to surrender any of the potential fruits of their joint endeavor. In the early days of most collective-bargaining relationships, the strike or the threat of a strike, as well as occasional use of the lockout, were the frequently ready means of settling even minor issues arising during the life of a labor agreement.

As most collective-bargaining relationships matured, however, the responsible representatives of both parties realized that the strike and the lockout are costly mechanisms. On any hard-headed factual appraisal it does not make sense to shut down a plant over most grievance issues with the resultant heavy losses to the company and to employees. The parties also found that too frequent use of the strike or lockout blunted the effectiveness of these economic weapons for potential use in more important controversies at the time of contract expiration.

These realities led to the gradual adoption of arbitration of grievances. The disadvantages of the strike and the lockout outweighed the strong reluctance to submit to outside intervention. The history of the development of arbitration is the subject matter of another paper in this series and will not be further discussed here. The basic fact which is important to this paper is that arbitration of grievances is an agreed-upon alternative to the strike and the lockout. The arbitration clause of a labor agreement is the price paid or the "swap" made for the no-strike, no-lockout clause. In the last analysis, arbitration will continue only so long as it serves its intended purpose. Will it continue to be preferable to the use of economic strength? Efforts to make this form of arbitration more acceptable are of more than academic interest.

The Significance of Voluntarism

In many respects, an agreement to arbitrate is basically the same as an agreement on any other subject. After weighing all the pros and cons, the parties have agreed to submit one or more present or unknown but potential disputes to a third party for decision. There is one very important difference in grievance arbitration. An agreement to arbitrate is an agreement to an unknown result; it is a venture of faith and hope. Because it is an agreement of this nature, it is not at all surprising that arbitration has been accepted reluctantly and only after unsatisfactory results with the use of economic weapons.

It is a fundamental thesis of this paper that the ultimate success or failure of arbitration during the term of an agreement depends in a substantial measure on the degree to which the unpredictables can be reduced so that the venture of faith and hope may rest on a firmer foundation.

Control of the Arbitration Process by the Parties

The first important element of voluntary arbitration is the selection of the arbitrator by mutual agreement. It is significant that both of the more important designating agencies (the American Arbitration Association and the Federal Mediation and Conciliation Service) have almost entirely discontinued their former practice of direct appointment of an arbitrator. They now submit lists of names from which the parties make a selection. In an increasing number of instances, the parties are selecting arbitrators by mutual agreement without the assistance of a designating agency. Where permanent arbitrators are named, it is customary to make a canvass of available persons and to make the final selection only after extensive exploration of information concerning these persons and their records. The basic principle that the arbitrator should be selected by mutual consent is essential to the system of voluntary arbitration. The act of selection of the arbitrator almost automatically brings the process one step closer to the parties.

More will be said later in this paper about the influence of the procedures of arbitration on its acceptability. The important point to be noted here is that in voluntary arbitration the parties make the choices as to place and time of hearing, method of presentation of the case, and the general climate of the proceedings. While these factors may appear to be relatively unimportant, they add up to a significant factor in appraising voluntary arbitration as against governmental or other forms of disputes settlement. The parties have the opportunity to shape the proceedings to their own needs.

A third important element of voluntary arbitration is the fact that the parties can define the extent and nature of the arbitrator's jurisdiction. It requires no elaborate examination of labor agreements to note the substantial differences on this point. Jurisdiction varies all the way from almost unlimited authority to severe limitations. Here again the parties have the opportunity to choose the type of arbitration they want.

In an effort to further minimize the unpredictable, some companies and unions mutually desire to participate in the development of a decision after the hearing. The formal method of accomplishing this purpose is the use of a tripartite arbitration board. Another method of securing the same result is through informal discussion of the issues and even of the decision between the arbitrator and responsible representatives of the parties after the hearing. On the other hand, some and probably most parties prefer that participation by the parties shall take place only at the hearing.

In all the ways noted above—(1) selection of the arbitrator, (2) control of the procedures, (3) determination of the arbitrator's jurisdiction, and (4) extent of participation by the parties in decision-making—the voluntary arbitration system presents a wide range of choice to the parties. It is an adaptable process, as is needed in an industrial relations climate which differs widely because of a variety of factors, including but not limited to:

a. Duration of the collective-bargaining relationship
b. Practices and mores of the industry or plant or geographical area
c. Dominant personalities in the ranks of both parties.

Implications of the "Final and Binding" Aspect of Voluntary Arbitration

Virtually all voluntary agreements to arbitrate include a clause in which both parties agree, in advance, to accept the award as a final and binding determination of the issue submitted. In one respect this clause is simply a necessary part of the swap for the no-strike, no-lockout clause. The arbitration clause would not be an adequate alternative to the strike or lockout if the award had only advisory status. The final and binding clause has an even deeper significance. When the parties place their signatures on the clause they assume a direct responsibility for the decisions issued. They may have bought a pig in a poke, but it was by their own choice that the purchase was made. In a very real sense, no decision is an imposed decision; each decision is a requested award.

Initial reactions to arbitration awards do not always lend support to the above assertion. However, such initial reactions usually give way as more mature reflection occurs. In the vast majority of relationships, the responsible parties support the sanctity of an award, however unpalatable it may be as an individual case. The system is considered more important than any one result of the system.

Despite the basic loyalty to their own commitments and the sense of good sportsmanship possessed by most company and union representatives, it is almost axiomatic that, in the overall picture, arbitration awards must be acceptable if the voluntary arbitration system is to survive. The too prevalent wildcat strikes arise because:

a. Employees in relatively new relationships have not lost enough by use of the strike weapon to realize the significance of the contractual bargain to use arbitration as an alternative; or

b. The issue is considered to be so important that employees deliberately violate the no-strike clause in the hope of securing short-run gains; or

c. Arbitration, as practiced, is not sufficiently acceptable to do the job intended.

The last reason is probably more frequently the true reason than is commonly admitted.

Unlike most personal or group relationships, collective bargaining is ordinarily a continuing relationship. Labor agreements cannot usually be discontinued after short periods of time as is the case in most commercial dealings. Collective bargaining has sometimes been compared to marriage, but even that comparison is not a valid one. There may have been a shotgun wedding at the outset as the result of a strike or an NLRB election, but divorce is unlikely. An arbitration award is necessarily injected into this continuing type of relationship where it will have an effect on the parties for an indefinite period of time. While awards can be modified by agreement of the parties themselves, experience indicates that it is even more difficult to change the terms of an award than to change a prior agreement of the parties. As a general proposition, awards are changed or modified by the parties only when they are quite unpalatable to both parties or are so objectionable to one party that they become a major issue at the time of the next contract negotiation. This lasting nature of awards makes reasonable acceptability even more important.

These characteristics of the collective-bargaining process and of arbitration awards issued under it require some examination of contract-grievance procedure of which arbitration is a part. Whether arbitration of grievances is listed in the contract under a separate heading or more specifically as the last step in the grievance procedure, it is a common feature of all contracts that arbitration is resorted to only after the issue has not been resolved at earlier stages of direct negotiation. What precedes arbitration?

The more important aims and purposes of mature grievance procedure may be listed as follows:

a. Collective bargaining continued—practical effectuation of the labor agreement by its application to specific plant problems.

b. The educational aim—development of knowledge of

and mutual respect for the positions and problems of each party.

c. The psychological aim—provision of a forum for the airing of complaints, real or alleged.

d. The preventive-maintenance aim—solving problems before they erupt into specific grievances.

There has been considerable discussion in recent years in industrial relations and arbitration circles of this basic concept: the function of making agreements by collective bargaining is by no means confined to the negotiation of a labor contract. Collective bargaining is a continuing process, with the grievance procedure playing a most important role. This position was summarized succinctly by George W. Taylor in an address before the National Academy of Arbitrators[1] on January 14, 1949, as follows:

> No sharp line can be drawn between agreement-making and agreement-administration. Grievance settlement involves not merely the application of clear and unmistakable agreement terms to individual cases but, particularly in the early stages of a relationship or as respects new terms added to an old contract, is also related to a completion of the agreement of the parties.

The validity of this assertion is readily demonstrable to anyone who has close day-by-day contacts with the grievance procedure. Virtually every clause of the contract is clarified or amplified by grievance settlements and, in addition, some grievance settlements create realistic collective-bargaining precedents on matters not even mentioned in the contract. Most of the clear-cut applications of the contract are disposed of at Step 1 or Step 2 of the grievance procedure. The bulk of the time and attention of the parties at later steps is devoted to the issues which are not clearly determinable by the language of the agreement itself.

An important by-product, if not a direct objective, of the grievance procedure is its educational value. Management representatives obtain new insight and value judgments of the problems and aspirations of employees and of the union

[1] Effectuating the Labor Agreement through Arbitration—Bureau of National Affairs.

as an organization. Union representatives learn to see and respect the problems of management. This educational objective is enhanced greatly by the fact that the process is not labeled as education. A shortcoming of most formal education is absent because the educational results are by-products of discussion of grievances which are live current issues.

A third aim of the grievance procedure is the opportunity afforded employees (also management representatives at times) to secure a forum in which their complaints may be aired. Complaints kept bottled up with no avenue for escape have created many dissatisfied and unsatisfactory employees. One does not have to be a student of psychology to appreciate the cathartic effect of the grievance procedure. This objective and result is not dependent on whether the complaint itself is valid. What is needed is exposure.

A fourth aim of the grievance procedure is to prevent grievances before they arise in specific form. The preventive-maintenance idea is fully accepted as respects plant and equipment. The engineering management which paints the roof only after it begins to leak, or greases the machine after it starts to squeak, has no place in industry today. Is it any less valid to design and administer the grievance procedure in a manner which will minimize or prevent the human squeaks before they develop?

If these are the basic aims and objectives of the grievance procedure, how does arbitration, the terminal point of the procedure, fit into the picture? Attempts will be made to answer this question in some detail later in this paper. At this point, however, it should be apparent that a grievance-arbitration system or procedure which ignores these aims and objectives, and is completely set apart from all that has transpired in discussion of the same grievance at earlier steps, will be far from acceptable. To be most effective, arbitration must strive to fulfill the objectives noted above.

The Arbitrator's Responsibilities and Limitations

The factor of risk to the parties in arbitration is often

underestimated, particularly by arbitrators. It is undoubtedly true that the stakes in a typical grievance arbitration are much smaller than in contract negotiation. However, there are exceptions. Lightly concealed under many seemingly innocuous grievances are fundamental principles which are of as much long-run significance to employees or to the company, or to both, as a general wage increase of several cents per hour. Dealing with some simple seniority cases, for example, is not unlike tinkering with the works of a wrist watch. As the scope of collective bargaining has enlarged, the issues presented to arbitration have become more difficult and technical. Some piece-work or work-standards cases, handled incompetently by an arbitrator, can be compared to retaining a plumber for an appendectomy. Under some pension systems, highly complicated actuarial problems may be presented to arbitration. Some risk is inherent and unavoidable as an integral part of the swap for a no-strike, no-lockout clause. It is imperative, however, that the risks be minimized.

The arbitrator necessarily decides most grievance cases with imperfect knowledge. He does not work in the plant. He has not followed the grievance throughout its course of development. Frequently he obtains only such information about the case as the parties choose to tell him in dressed-up fashion. In many instances the dressing up is so complete that is it difficult indeed to recognize the same animal under the two descriptions. In addition, the arbitrator may happen to be inexperienced in handling the type of issue presented. It is any wonder that decisions are written which are not acceptable?

Earlier in this monograph it was noted that the selection of the arbitrator by mutual agreement is an essential part of the voluntary arbitration system. This right of the parties to select obviously implies the right to reject before selection or to reject an arbitrator for further services after one or more ad hoc cases or after long or short service as a permanent arbitrator. It has been suggested that some companies and unions exercise these rights with little concern for the arbitrator, and that formal or informal white lists or black lists are developed out of capricious or even malicious motives. It is held that these lists are often compiled on the basis of the number of cases won and lost with little consideration for the merit or lack of merit in the awards. Although there may be some element of truth in these suggestions, and although improvements in the selection process may not be amiss in some quarters, the writer is of the considered opinion that under a voluntary arbitration system the arbitrator necessarily has no rights beyond the tenure of his specific appointment. Confidence in the arbitrator is an essential ingredient to acceptability of his awards. Once that confidence of the parties is lost, whether for good reasons or even for foolish or improper ones, the usefulness of the arbitrator is at an end. The system is more important than the individual arbitrator, and the likelihood that he will be rejected is a part of the arbitrator's occupational job description. Loss of confidence is not synonymous with dissatisfaction with specific awards although a build-up of a series of such instances may have that result. Real loss of confidence is often an intangible result, recognizable but not definable.

The arbitrator may not be the only casualty of the selection process. Because of the knowledge limitations of the arbitrator, noted earlier, the parties need to educate every new arbitrator to the intricacies of their contract, their plant, and their own special practices and mores. This educational process may be expensive in arbitration fees, in time required for case preparation, in time of representatives paid for by the parties at hearings, and in unacceptable decisions based on inadequate knowledge. In a very real sense, the parties make a financial investment in the education of every different arbitrator.

Is arbitration a profession? That question is largely academic and deserves little attention here. There does exist some difference of opinion among persons in the labor relations field as to the relative merit or lack of merit in selecting professional arbitrators (persons who devote the major portion of their time to arbitration) in contrast to individuals who have some other regular gainful occupation and do only a limited amount of arbitration work on a part-time basis. No precise data are available as to the distribution of arbitrators on this basis. From such limited information as is available, the writer would estimate that labor arbitrators in the United States serving as arbitrators under voluntary arbitration arrangements could be divided in groups as follows:

Group	*Approximate Number*	*Description*
A	30	Persons working relatively full time with arbitration as their sole gainful occupation.
B	150	Persons performing a substantial amount of arbitration work who have some other regular gainful occupation.
C	More than 1000	Persons performing a limited amount of arbitration work (estimated at from one to ten cases per year).

If the rough estimates indicated above are translated into volume of cases decided, it is probable that the small group of approximately thirty full-time arbitrators (Group A) handle almost half as many total cases per year as the group of approximately 150 arbitrators in Group B. It is reasonably certain that the Group A and Group B arbitrators together handle more total cases per year than the Group C arbitrators. In short, the Group A and Group B men, totaling about 180 persons, are performing more than half the total case-load per year. Although no satisfactory data are available for earlier periods in the history of arbitration, is it reasonably certain that the picture was different as late as ten years ago. The full-time arbitrator was then a rarity. Most arbitrators decided only an occasional case. If Group A arbitrators and some part of the Group B arbitrators are considered as the professional arbitrators, it is apparent that a professional group is emerging, whatever may be the theories on the subject.

My acquaintanceship with other arbitrators indicates that men in Groups B and C retain other gainful occupations for a variety of reasons. Many are teachers, lawyers, etc., who have a genuine interest in arbitration aside from its monetary aspects. If forced to choose between arbitration and their other regular occupation, however, they would confine themselves to the latter, entirely as a matter of personal preference. Others would make the same choice, but because the security risks and expendability characteristics of arbitration are too ominous. Still others would become Group A arbitrators without hesitation if they could secure enough business to justify the change in employment status. On the other side of the picture, Group A arbitrators occasionally fall out of that classification because they have become partially expended for one reason or another or because they find other work more agreeable.

It is my opinion that this situation is a generally healthy one. The process of selection by mutual agreement may be rough and ready, but it provides the voluntary system with alternatives. If the parties desire professional arbitrators, they are available or can be created out of Group C men. If they desire nonprofessional arbitrators there is no lack of material.

No fully satisfactory methods have been developed for training arbitrators. The trial-and-error method is one which may be costly to the parties in terms of inadequate decisions born out of inexperience. And potentially excellent arbitrators may be and have been killed off by a single unfortunate incident. Moreover, there are few good methods by which a prospective arbitrator may break in. If a large number of persons had not obtained related experience during World War II through service with the War Labor Board, the parties to collective bargaining would by this time be facing a most acute shortage of qualified arbitrators. Some colleges and universities are attempting to meet the training need by courses directly or indirectly designed to provide essential background knowledge. Probably the best method (some form of apprenticeship with an experienced arbitrator) is difficult to effectuate because the full-time arbitrators are few, and in many cases the nature of their practice does not lend itself to satisfactory use of apprenticeship assistance.

The future of labor arbitration depends in no small measure on the exhibited competence and integrity of the practitioners. Can arbitrators measure up to the requirements? I believe that the system can survive, but that it may not survive unless all parties at interest (companies, unions, and arbitrators) give more considered attention to improving the acceptability of the process.

Differences in Basic Concepts Held by the Parties

Reference has already been made to one of the virtues of voluntary arbitration—its flexibility. The process can be adapted to a variety of collective-bargaining situations and to different stages of development. This virtue is dependent, however, on both the company and the union, signatories to the same agreement, having a common point of view about the kind of arbitration they want and have bargained for. The most legalistic type of arbitration is thoroughly defensible if both parties consistently want it.

Reasonably extensive experience in arbitration under a wide variety of arbitration clauses makes it apparent to me that a real meeting of the minds on the type of arbitration desired has not been achieved in many instances. Because of the rapid expansion of grievance arbitration, many arbitration clauses have been copied out of some other contract with no clear idea by either party as to the meaning of the clause. In other cases, the arbitration clause once had clear meaning to the parties, but they have long since gone down other roads in developing their grievance and arbitration practices. The language of the outmoded clause is occasionallly trotted out in particular cases when it is considered possible to gain a tactical advantage by doing so. In still other cases, strong points of view are held with reasonable consistency by both parties, but they are different. The contract arbitration clause may be a poorly designed compromise. Or the language may essentially support the position of one party, but the other party may seek to break down the clause because it was never really accepted or understood.

The matter is further complicated by the fact that many companies and unions understandably adopt inconsistent positions, depending on the case being arbitrated. For a number of years I served as arbitrator under a contract which contained a very restrictive arbitration clause. The company would generally object vigorously to instances in which it believed that the umpire was overstepping his authority. It was not uncommon, however, to encounter cases in which the company position could be summarized as follows:

> We realize that the union has us "over the barrel" by strict application of contract language. But we never intended this result, and the union position is unreasonable and inequitable. This request has ominous implications. After all, we have to operate the plant. Please be a reasonable man and dismiss the grievance.

In that case, and despite its general dissatisfaction with the restrictive arbitration clause, the union position could be summarized as follows:

> Never mind the equities or reasonableness of this request. The function of the umpire is limited to strict application of the agreement language.

In an opposite type of case, perhaps heard the very same day, the essential positions of both parties would be reversed.

In short, the arbitrator under many agreements faces problems arising out of a combination of a lack of reasonable meeting of the minds as to basic intent of the arbitration clause plus an understandable tendency of the parties to shift positions depending on the case being arbitrated. In this situation, the permanent arbitrator, and to only slightly lesser extent the ad hoc arbitrator, is often forced into the position of having to interpret the arbitration clause itself as a necessary prelude to deciding the specific issue before him.

The fundamental differences in basic thinking about grievance arbitration can be summarized by contrasting the concept of solving problems against the concept of winning battles. But this is an over-simplification. The next chapter is an attempt to explore in more detail the relevance of various procedures and methods of grievance arbitration to the acceptability concept and to attempt to point up to the parties the need for more complete meeting of the minds as to the kind of arbitration desired.

RELATIONSHIP BETWEEN ACCEPTABILITY AND BASIC CONCEPTS OF THE PARTIES AS REFLECTED IN PROCEDURES AND TYPES OF ARBITRATION SYSTEMS

The Climate of the Hearing and the Presentation of Evidence

The establishment of a suitable climate for the arbitration hearing begins with the physical arrangement and location of the hearing-room. Most parties have found that the conference table set-up is the most satisfactory arrangement. Sufficient space is provided for note-taking and for availability of materials needed in case presentation. The scene is comparable to the preceding step of the grievance procedure except for the arbitrator at the head of the table. The traditional courtroom arrangement is not as satisfactory. It is more uncomfortable, more formal, and puts the arbitrator in an elevated spot which he does not deserve or enjoy, figuratively or literally.

I have observed some change of practice in recent years with respect to location of the hearing-room. Some years ago there was frequent insistence, particularly by unions, on holding the hearing at a so-called neutral location such as a hotel meeting-room. Some part of this insistence may have been due to a feeling that the impartial nature of the proceedings would be given psychological impetus by meeting off company property. In any event, more practical considerations now usually govern the determination. Hearings on company property are frequent because of the cost factor, the ready availability of representatives and witnesses, the advantage of quick access to records, and the ready possibility of visiting the location of the job or the scene of the incident. Hearings are ordinarily held off company property only when adequate space and facilities there are unavailable or when there is a likelihood of frequent interruptions if the parties are too close to the daily job. As a general proposition, most parties want the hearing at a location most accessible to the majority of the participants.

The Principal Spokesman

A more important consideration is the selection by the parties of their own spokesmen at the hearing. As a practical necessity, some one person on each side of the table must assume the responsibility of organizing and perhaps taking the leading part in presenting the case. Opinions differ widely as to choice of the principal spokesman.

Some parties prefer to have the case presented primarily by the person in the local union or in the local plant personnel office who took the leading part in the discussion at the earlier steps of the grievance procedure. This has obvious advantages. These persons know the complete history of the grievance. They are in a position to answer most questions authoritatively. Most significant, the assumption of major responsibility by these persons properly enhances their true importance in the grievance-settling process. The psychological aim and the educational aim of the grievance procedure, noted earlier in this paper, are fulfilled. As a more indirect but nonetheless realistic result, such presentation minimizes the possibility of passing the buck to others if the case is lost. Local union and company representatives may proceed more constructively in future grievance settlement, or more carefully in screening future cases for arbitration. There are disadvantages. Local union or local plant representatives sometimes lack the ability to organize and present a clear case to an arbitrator, even though they are fully competent to argue the case at earlier stages of the procedure. The necessity to educate an outsider imposes an additional burden, not present when the participants all know the background of the dispute, the contract terms, and their prior applications. An additional insufficiency may arise in a multi-plant agreement or even under a single-plant agreement because the local representatives may not be fully aware of practices and policy as applied elsewhere.

Another practice frequently observed by companies or unions is to choose as the major spokesman a representative from the main office of the company or from the International Union. This practice has advantages and disadvantages largely in reverse order from those noted above. The best spokesmen in this category fully utilize local personnel for presentation of the evidence.

A particularly touchy subject is the use or non-use of attorneys at grievance-arbitration proceedings. Legal training does present the possibility of making more orderly and persuasive arguments than is typical of persons without such training or its equivalent. However, attorneys have serious limitations in these proceedings. Ordinarily they are not sufficiently familiar with the practical realities of the case to present a full picture. Because their information is secondhand it becomes third-hand by the time the arbitrator receives it, and it is often passed on by an attorney who is not much more familiar with the real situation than is the arbitrator. In many instances the lawyer is much more interested in winning the case to demonstrate his prowess than in solving an industrial relations problem. I have no prejudice against use of attorneys by either companies or unions, but I have observed that the really effective attorneys are those who are primarily labor-relations men and attorneys secondarily. Such attorneys can be constructive. Ordinarily they confine their activities to organization of the case and discussion of such legal concepts as may be relevant. Deliberately and conscientiously, they call on other company or union representatives for actual presentation of most of the evidence.

One general observation can be made. Regardless of the identity of the principal spokesman for either side, he can be more constructive if he has participated in the grievance step just preceding arbitration.

It is also my considered opinion that many companies and unions tend to underestimate the value of employee or supervisory testimony, and overestimate the importance to the case of the principal spokesmen. I recall a case in which the hearing of a piece-rate dispute had continued for some time and the closing arguments had finally been made. On the basis of the evidence submitted, the union had a hopeless case. A little girl sitting at the back of the room (an operator on the job) could contain herself no longer. She interrupted with a simple nine-word sentence. That sentence was so important that, after the confirmation of its validity, the union won the case.

Methods of Case Presentation

Underlying the choice of the principal spokesman there often exists a more important consideration. Earlier in this paper it was noted that many presentations in arbitration are so dressed up that the two versions have little resemblance to each other. There is an understandable tendency for each party to overemphasize its strong arguments and to ignore or unduly belittle the weak points. There may be instances where these tactics are successful in winning a case because the other party is not sufficiently on its toes to make a good presentation. However, cases won in this fashion are not problems solved, nor do they enhance the acceptability of arbitration. It is my considered opinion that most arbitrators react most favorably to the presentations when each party frankly lines up the strong points and the weak points in its case and argues the case on the basis of the weight of evidence. If both parties follow this course, shadow boxing is minimized and more acceptable decisions are obtained.

This sort of case presentation by a party may lose cases on occasion, but the ones lost should be lost. I recall a seniority case under a "when abilities are approximately equal, seniority governs" clause. The company had promoted the junior employee. The company attorney presented a long argument, and then confidently called on the immediate supervisor of the two employees and asked him to compare their abilities. The brief answer, "Oh, I guess they're about six of one and a half dozen of the other," collapsed the company case. But the purpose of the grievance procedure had been fulfilled. The major point of this incident, and of the earlier one involving the nine-word sentence testimony of the operator, is that both parties can become so steamed up about the theories and principles of a case that they may ignore the operating realities. It is also obvious in these two instances that the earlier steps of the grievance procedure had not been satisfactory.

A second and related matter dealing with case presentation is the method of utilizing witnesses. Some parties prefer the question-and-answer method. My observation is that this method is much less satisfactory than a simple request of the witness to tell his story in his own way. The occasional witness may become long-winded and irrelevant and may have to be curbed if he becomes overenthusiastic in his presentation, but the average witness gets his story across in much less time and with a far greater sense of satisfaction if he is not restricted to answering questions. It sometimes happens that such a witness lets the cat out of the bag when carefully devised questions might have kept it concealed. If that happens, it is all to the good in the light of the larger objectives of the grievance procedure. And for every time that a case is spoiled by a naïve witness, the same type of testimony will win another case.

Briefs

There is a wide variety of practice with respect to presentation of briefs to the arbitrator. In some procedures, briefs of any variety are virtually unknown. At the opposite extreme, some parties almost invariably present briefs before or at the hearing as well as after the hearing. Not infrequently they also file reply briefs.

A brief prepared for presentation sometime prior to the hearing is requested by some arbitrators or is desired by the parties in the belief that information about the case prior to the hearing will facilitate understanding of the issues by the arbitrator and sharpen the proceedings at the hearing. I prefer to go into a case cold, believing that the oral and visual elements of the hearing produce a more valid overall impression than the written word, and that it is advisable to enter a hearing without any preformed ideas on the merits of the issue. An objection to pre-hearing briefs sometimes made by one or both parties is that they do not want to disclose their arguments and evidence to the other party prior to the hearing. This position seems to me to be worse than valueless. It implies that an arbitration proceeding is a game, and not a proceeding resorted to after all reasonable efforts at direct negotiation have failed.

Briefs prepared by the parties and submitted to the arbitrator either prior to or at the hearing do have a number of values. First and foremost, the preparation of a thorough brief should force a company or a union to think through the implications of its position, perhaps for the first time. If the other party does likewise, the preparation of the briefs may in itself be a strong motivating force toward settlement of the grievance prior to arbitration. Secondly, preparation of a brief tends toward a more orderly and a shorter hearing. Finally, the basic facts and arguments, as the parties see them, are presented in a manner which relieves the arbitrator of some of the burden of note-taking at the hearing if a verbatim transcript is not taken.

The principal disadvantage of briefs is that the reducing of a position to writing sometimes has an effect opposite to the achievement of a settlement. It may harden and formalize the position of the parties, making it more difficult for them to recede from those positions and more difficult for them to accept an award. It is often the case that a person is more carried away by the induced eloquence of his written words than by a dozen speeches. The speech may act as a cathartic. The written word tends to freeze the idea. For these reasons, as well as the practical one of the time and work required for brief preparation, many parties prefer not to file briefs.

It is my opinion that post-hearing briefs usually have less value than briefs prepared before the hearing. They may be valuable and in fact necessary if some phase of the testimony at the hearing requires the submission of additional or more extensive evidence, and the parties agree to submit that evidence in the form of briefs or letters rather than at a continuation of the oral hearing. But in an ordinary case, when the parties concede that all the pertinent evidence is in at the hearing, a post-hearing brief tends to be only a rehash, and simply acts to delay the decision. The only conceivable value of such briefs is to lighten the arbitrator's burden of note-taking. There is not much help even on this score, since the arbitrator cannot be certain that the briefs will contain all the significant testimony and evidence. Irrespective of any personal ideas on the subject, the insistence of either or both parties in filing a post-hearing brief within a reasonable time after the hearing and exchanged with the other party should be respected by the arbitrator.

Transcripts

The taking of a verbatim transcript at the hearing is frequently insisted on by arbitrators or by one or both of the parties in important new contract cases, but the practice is much less prevalent in grievance proceedings. Most arbitrators adapt themselves to the wishes of the parties in this particular. In favor of the practice is the fact that an accurate transcript is of considerable value to the arbitrator in making certain that the positions of the parties are understood accurately, in securing an accurate background of the case, and in picking up evidence that appeared to be largely irrelevant at the time it was given, but assumes significance in the light of later developments at the hearing. The laborious duty of extensive note-taking by the arbitrator at the hearing may dull his sense of perception. The parties sometimes want a transcript in order to check up on the arbitrator to make sure that he omits no important points in his consideration of the case. On the other side of the picture, cost to the parties is the principal deterrent. Another objection sometimes made is that witnesses, and particularly employee witnesses, will be afraid to talk if a transcript is taken. My observation is that this objection is not a very realistic one in most situations, especially after the parties become accustomed to the presence of a reporter. The opposite tendency is more likely. There is some inclination to talk for the record.

Plant Visitations

In a substantial number of cases, acceptability of an award is materially enhanced if the arbitrator visits the work place or the scene of an incident. The eye is better than the ear in many aspects of disputes, or at least is a valuable supplement to oral or written evidence. A plant visit is a simple device by which the arbitrator can secure a better understanding of the background of a case. In some instances a plant visit either before or during the hearing will serve to avoid voluminous testimony. The award may be more realistic and therefore acceptable because the plant visit fills part of the gap in the arbitrator's knowledge. There may also be a valuable subsidiary contribution to acceptability. Employees on the job, but not at the hearing, will tend to think more of the arbitrator's judgment if they know that he has taken the trouble to get at least that close to the environment in which they work every day.

While some of the above considerations are not major items in their relationship to the acceptability concept, the sum total of all these factors may make a vital difference, particularly to employees, in whether arbitration is conceived of as a distant, abstract, and unsatisfactory substitute for the strike, or as a friendly, down-to-reality procedure in which they have a significant part.

Types of Arbitration

The grievance-arbitration scene today presents a wide variation of types of arbitration. However, there are trends discernible over recent periods which are significant in terms of the subject matter of this paper.

Tenure (Ad Hoc vs. *Permanent Arbitrator)*

One major difference in voluntary arbitration systems is the decision made by the parties as to tenure of their arbitrator. At the one extreme are those companies and unions that rarely select the same arbitrator twice. At the other extreme is the infrequent situation in which the same arbitrator serves the same parties for a period of ten years or longer. The simple contrasting of these extremes is the best evidence of the diversity in acceptability of arbitration and of arbitrators.

Ad hoc arbitration remains as the most prevalent practice in terms of the numbers of labor contracts. Defined briefly, ad hoc arbitration exists when the parties do not select an arbitrator in advance, but make a selection with or without the assistance of a designating agency *after* a case or a group of cases has been appealed to arbitration. The selection is made only for that case or group of cases. There is no obligation to use the same arbitrator again.

So-called permanent arbitration exists when the parties select an arbitrator or arbitrators for then unknown unsettled grievances (if any arise) which may require arbitration in the future. The period of advance selection usually is the life of the labor agreement, almost never longer. It may be for a shorter period (i.e., a six-month period in one known contract). Or the arbitrator may be selected in advance but with the stipulated right of either or both parties to seek his removal at any time. In all instances, the distinguishing feature is that the selection is made in advance of the appeal of specific cases to arbitration. It is a popular misconception that permanent arbitrators are retained on a full-time basis by one company and one union. That does happen in a few of the larger set-ups, but permanent arbitrators who work on a part-time basis in any one set-up are even more common. It is obvious that the adjective "permanent" is a misnomer. It is rare indeed that "permanent" arbitrators are really permanent in the sense that they serve for a lifetime or for a long period of years.

The trend is unmistakably in the direction of permanent arbitration. As late as 1940, permanent arbitrators were largely confined to a few of the more mature collective-bargaining relationships such as men's clothing, the dress industry, and some parts of the textile industry. Since that time many large companies and unions in such mass production industries as automobiles, rubber, steel, meat packing, shipbuilding, and agricultural implements have adopted some form of permanent arbitration system. Moreover, even under the ad hoc systems there is some discernible tendency for companies and unions to continue to select the same arbitrator for a series of cases, thus obtaining the rough equivalent of permanent arbitration systems. On the alternative bases of total number of decisions issued or numbers of employees covered by the two types of arbitration, it is probably a close question whether ad hoc arbitration still maintains a dominant position. Does this trend have any relevance to the subject matter of this paper? The writer believes that it does. In a pamphlet[1] prepared jointly by the writer and Van D. Kennedy in 1946, we listed the advantages and disadvantages of the two types of tenure. The advantages of each system as obtained from that source are repeated here with minor modifications:

Advantages of "Permanent" Tenure

a. The arbitrator gradually becomes familiar with, and eventually expert in, the contract clauses, wage-payment plans, industrial techniques, and processes of the industry.

b. Decisions will tend to be consistent one with another. Because of this, precedents will be established, the parties will know what

[1] *Arbitration of Grievances,* U. S. Department of Labor, Division of Labor Standards, 1946.

to expect from the arbitrator, and similar cases in the future are more likely to be resolved by agreement at an early stage of the grievance procedure. It is pointless to whip a dead horse by pushing a second time the same type of grievance which has been lost once.

c. No time is lost in choosing an arbitrator after the initial selection. Less time is usually consumed in making arrangements for hearings. The grievance procedure is shortened to the advantage of both parties, particularly in discharge or seniority cases where an employee's job status is in doubt and back pay may be involved.

d. The permanent arbitrator becomes acquainted with the personalities on both sides of the table.

e. As a result of (a) and (d) above, time required for the presentation of evidence at hearings is shortened substantially. The parties do not have to educate the arbitrator each time, and there is less tendency for one or both parties to stray from the subject at hand or belabor a point.

f. The permanent arbitrator requires less time for investigation and preparation of opinions due to familiarity with the industry and with the parties.

g. The permanent arbitrator is less likely to require a verbatim transcript.

h. As a result of (e), (f), and (g) above, the direct cost of each arbitration (fees and expenses of the arbitrator and expense of a transcript, if taken) and the indirect costs (time spent by the representatives of the parties and the union or company cost for time of witnesses, etc.) are usually less than for a series of temporary arbitrators.

i. There is less tendency for either party to throw in a few admittedly weak cases with the thought that a green arbitrator will split the difference and by this means give favorable decisions on the more important cases, or even give favorable decisions on some of the weak cases.

j. The arbitrator must live with the parties and with his own decisions. He cannot blithely toss off a decision, knowing that he may never see the parties again. A really bad decision may come back to haunt him. If any emphasis on responsibility is needed, tenure provides it.

k. When a permanent arbitrator can secure the full confidence of both parties, they may sometimes request him to step out of his semi-judicial role and assist them in the mediation of potential disputes.

Advantages of Ad Hoc Arbitration

a. This system permits easy change of the third party if the arbitrator proves to be incompetent.
b. It facilitates selection of an arbitrator especially qualified for the grievance dispute in question. For example, the parties can judge the experience and qualifications of prospective arbitrators in handling disputes over incentive pay.
c. It is well adapted to situations where arbitration is an entirely new idea to both parties and they wish to experiment, or where experience has shown that practically all disputes can be resolved by the parties.
d. An ad hoc arbitration system does not eliminate the possibility of continuous reselection of the same individual, thus securing many of the benefits of a permanent system without some of its liabilities.

The risk factor in arbitration is reduced by permanent tenure. The arbitrator has fewer knowledge limitations. There is less unpredictability in the process. These are potent factors tending toward greater acceptability, and it seems evident that the parties have been moving toward permanent arbitration for these reasons.

Systems Utilizing a Single Arbitrator

The second major difference in systems of arbitration is use of a single arbitrator or some type of arbitration board. The single arbitrator is by far the most prevalent system for arbitration of grievances. This is in some contrast to new-contract or contract-wage-reopening cases where an arbitration board is much more likely to be established.

The words most commonly used to characterize a single arbitrator are: arbitrator, umpire, or impartial chairman. (Less glamorous or more inelegant words may be used sometimes by the parties in private conversation, but these can be left to the imagination.) In actual practice, there is little necessary relevance between the title given to the arbitrator by the parties and their concept of his function. However, the words do have different meanings, at least in theory; and for purposes of this section of this paper, the three titles will be considered as having meaning in themselves.

Since it is the generic term, the title of arbitrator may be used and is used with almost any type of system. Its most common meaning, however, is the ad hoc or temporary arbitrator already discussed.

The umpire title (also the less-frequently used title of referee) obviously originates from the national pastimes in which these titles are used. It infers a limited type of jurisdiction, calling "balls and strikes," etc., under rigid and rather exact rules. It is most commonly associated with the type of contract which limits jurisdiction to findings of violation or non-violation of the agreement, and interpretation and application. As originally conceived, the idea was that the umpire's responsibilities would not be creative in any respect. Nor would there be compromise decisions. Even the closest ones would have to be called one way or the other. These original ideas concerning the umpire system almost always break down to some extent. However, the title of umpire remains in common use, and the parties using that title ordinarily retain at least some elements of the ideas associated originally with the title.

The term "impartial chairman" has quite a different connotation. Ordinarily, the impartial chairman is not chairman of any formal board. In essence, he is a chairman of a continued grievance meeting, brought in by voluntary act of the parties to help them find a solution to a common problem after they have been unable to agree. He is usually expected to mediate if mediation is possible. But he has an added responsibility, the duty and obligation to decide the case if a mediated settlement is not obtainable. As is the case with use of the other titles, an impartial chairman is not always expected to pursue a course of action implied by his title. In some instances, the parties call the arbitrator their impartial chairman, but what they really want and expect is an umpire.

Since the actual practice in grievance arbitration today is to be quite inexact about use of titles, most of the discussion in the later portions of this paper will be in terms of the basic concepts which may underlie these titles and are obviously of much greater importance than any handle which may be affixed to an arbitrator. However, it may be observed in passing that more precise use of titles might help the parties and arbitrators to a better understanding of the kind of arbitration expected.

Arbitration Boards

The type of arbitration board most in use is the tripartite board composed of one representative of each party and a third member whose title may be any one of the titles discussed in the preceding section. There are many advantages of a tripartite board. The principal one is that the risks of arbitration can be reduced substantially. If such a board functions as intended, i.e., by joint discussion of a case up to the final point of issuance of a decision with realistic appraisal of their own cases by the party representatives, the major risk in arbitration (lack of adequate knowledge on the part of the arbitrator) is materially lessened. There is an additional advantage directly pertaining to the acceptability concept. Concurrence by one or both of the party representatives in an award which is often a modification of the official position taken by one or both parties carries with it an obligation of the company or union or both to give active support to the award. Moreover, it is no secret that many dissents are for the record, and the award is, in reality, a negotiated solution.

In theory, I should prefer to function in a tripartite arbitration board in each and every case, no matter how trivial the issue may appear to be. However, there are very practical disadvantages. The cost to the parties of this type of grievance arbitration is necessarily much greater than for a single arbitrator, and is often so great that it is not a realistic system. Unfortunately an additional major disadvantage is that the party representatives may simply rehash the same old arguments. They are not permitted to take a realistic position publicly, and in some instances are not even permitted to take their hair down privately. If this is the case, the major purpose of the tripartite board is absent, and the only result is a costly, time-consuming procedure. In fairness to the party representatives, it should be added that many arbitrators also misunderstand the true purpose of a tripartite board and give them little opportunity to be effective. The extreme of this observation exists in known cases where the neutral board member has walked into the first and only board meeting with a fully prepared decision and has tossed it on the table with the question: "Well, who is going to vote with me?"

An additional possible disadvantage, often stressed, is that if a majority vote is required, the neutral arbitrator may have to modify his position so drastically to secure a majority that the decision is a bad decision. This danger undoubtedly exists, but it is my personal opinion that it is overemphasized. The opposite side of the coin is that if the arbitrator is unable to persuade anybody of the soundness of his position, it may very well be that that position needs serious reëxamination. And if both party representatives are so unreasonable that a fair decision cannot be obtained, the neutral arbitrator always has as an ace in the hole the possibility of withdrawing from the proceedings with no decision being issued. If that ace has to be turned up, it usually results in an award.

A seldom-used device in grievance arbitration is an all-neutral member board of three or more persons, all serving on the same case. Its only purpose is to secure a wider range of experience, knowledge, and points of view than is possible in selection of a single arbitrator. The cost factor makes this device unsatisfactory except for cases of major importance.

A more common type of all-neutral member board is a variety of permanent arbitration system under which two or more persons are named as arbitrators on a board or panel. They actually serve as single arbitrators on individual cases, and are selected by the parties for specific cases either in rotation or by successive elimination of some members for that case.

A third system is in reality not an arbitration board. It is the selection of a single arbitrator, but with one or more other arbitrators also selected as deputy or associate arbitrators. This system is confined almost solely to permanent arbitration systems where the desired "first man" does not have enough time available to give full time to the job, or where the case load is so heavy that assistance is required. The essential difference between this system and the panel system noted above is that there is a recognized first man and a recognized second man (deputy or associate). This system actually works in one of two ways. The deputy arbitrator may have only assistant status, and his work is confined largely to the spade work in handling cases. The first man is expected to hear all or most cases and to accept full responsibility for all decisions. Under the other method, the two men work as approximate equals, with full authority granted to both of them by the parties. The difference between the first man and the second man is that the former is expected to serve on the most important cases, and the two consult each other on most decisions. After some extensive service both as second man and first man under both varieties of this system, I believe that there are many advantages. One of the important advantages to arbitration generally is that it is the best form of apprenticeship training. The advantage to the parties is that there is more flexibility in the arrangement than with a single arbitrator. In instances of illness or temporary unavailability of one man, the other is likely to be available. Temporary peak loads of cases can be handled more expeditiously. And if one arbitrator resigns, there is no necessary time gap before a new arbitrator becomes familiar with the industry.

Jurisdiction

It is a basic consideration in all questions involving jurisdiction that limitations on the arbitrator's authority which are imposed by the parties stem from three principal sources. The first is the risk element in arbitration. This includes fear of the competence or integrity of the arbitrator or arbitrators generally. The second is the fear of the parties that genuine collective bargaining will be enervated if too ready access to arbitration is provided. The third is the general reluctance of both parties to relinquish authority on matters which they consider to be vital to their sovereignty or to their very existence. Thus some jurisdictional limitations are reflections on the state of the art of arbitration and are not really matters of principle. Others are real or alleged matters of principle.

Jurisdiction of the arbitrator can be considered most conveniently under two headings:

1. Limitations on subject matter.
2. Limitations on exercise of discretion within subject matters admittedly within the arbitrator's jurisdiction.

Specific Limitations on Subject Matter

Jurisdictional limitations on subject matter as found in a variety of contracts are both specific and general. Specific limitations may be illustrated by the following clauses taken from agreements:

Example No. 1 (large rubber company)

Specifically, the umpire shall not have the power to arbitrate general wage levels.

Example No. 2 (large rayon company)

The arbitrator shall not have the authority to change negotiated wage scales or negotiated typical job assignments.

Few generalizations can be made about the coverage of specific limitations. About the only semi-universal limitation is the one illustrated by the first clause quoted above. The grievance arbitrator is almost never permitted to arbitrate the general level of wages. Even this one generalization has an exception. There are some contracts in which a wage-reopening clause of the contract is made subject to the jurisdiction of the grievance arbitrator. However, in these instances the parties have really decided that their arbitrator may serve in two capacities—as grievance arbitrator, and in a separate realm as arbitrator under the wage-reopening clause. Despite the dual role in these few exceptional cases, the generalization holds good. The grievance arbitrator, as such, does not arbitrate general wage levels.

A related subject matter is usually outside the arbitrator's authority. In addition to general wage levels, the majority of contracts provide that if there is a negotiated rate for a job, and if there has been no change in the job since the rate was negotiated, the arbitrator may not alter the rate. These are the so-called rate inequality cases. This type of specific limitation is illustrated by the second clause quoted above. In that same contract there are other provisions about changed jobs which are subject to the arbitrator's jurisdiction.

Beyond the two subject matters noted above (general wage levels and alleged job rate inequalities), specific limitations, if any exist, vary so widely between contracts that little more can be said about them. With no necessary significance to the order in which they are recorded, and with no attempt to be inclusive, the following items may be mentioned as items sometimes outside the jurisdiction of the grievance arbitrator:

a. Production standards on hourly rated jobs.

b. Actual determination of piece rates (as distinguished from principles of piece work determination).

c. Questions involving medical judgments (disability under pension plans or under clauses providing for pay over and above compensation benefits).

d. The establishment of pension or insurance plans, or the determination of issues under such plans which involve actuarial problems.

Even a glance at these specific limitations indicates that they arise out of some combination of the three basic considerations noted at the beginning of this section. The matter of general wage levels involves all three (risk, possible enervation of collective bargaining, and sovereignty). On the other hand, a limitation involving a medical issue is almost solely due to one factor in the risk element in arbitration, the knowledge limitation of the arbitrator. With the probable exception of the changed job vs. job rate inequality type of case, specific limitations on the arbitrator's authority do not present much of a problem to arbitrators. Ordinarily the parties understand the specific limitations of their agreement.

General Limitations on Subject Matter

The most difficult jurisdiction problems arise out of the general limitations which are contained in many agreements. In the course of preparing this paper, the writer has examined the arbitration clauses of some seventy-five agreements in a variety of industries. This sample is much too small to justify quantitative conclusions. However, it is sufficiently representative to permit some generalizations and to supply illustrative examples.

It is a popular but mistaken idea that broad jurisdiction is given to the arbitrator in only a very few long-established relationships. There does appear to be some correlation between the granting of extensive jurisdiction and the duration of collective bargaining, but this is not an infallible rule by any means. Several relatively new contracts in industries such as shipbuilding, rubber, and steel contain arbitration clauses giving extensive jurisdiction to the arbitrator despite the predominance of restrictive clauses in these industries. Conversely, some contracts in industries such as the textile industry contain restrictive clauses despite the general tendency toward broad jurisdiction. It appears that the type of jurisdiction conferred on the arbitrator depends on a number of factors such as:

a. Duration of the collective-bargaining relationship in the industry or plant involved.

b. Position of the union on the jurisdiction issue.

c. Position of the employer or employers generally in that industry or geographical area on the jurisdiction issue.

d. Type of jurisdiction clause favored by legal advisors to the employer.

Examples of broad jurisdiction are indicated as follows:

Example No. 1 (medium-size rubber company)

All grievances on the part of the employees shall be disposed of in the following manner except that disputes on general wage increases shall not be subject to arbitration.

Example No. 2 (street railway company)

Should any difference arise between the Company and the Association, as to the true intent and meaning of any provision of this Agreement, or any other question which may arise between the parties hereto, which cannot be mutually and amicably adjusted . . .

Example No. 3 (men's clothing area agreement)

All grievances and disputes arising in the shops . . .

Another interesting example of broad jurisdiction is found in the following agreement terms of a shipbuilding contract:

(1) The Union or the Corporation may present to the Adjustment Board any complaint which either party may have of any violation by the other party of any of the terms and provisions of this Agreement and it shall be the duty of the Adjustment Board to receive and consider and decide on the merits of any such complaint and to order any adjustment within the scope and terms of this Agreement which may be adjudged by the Board to be proper.
(2) All complaints, disputes or grievances between the Corporation and the Union concerning matters beyond the scope or terms of this Agreement, which cannot be settled promptly shall be submitted to arbitration upon the demand in writing of either the Corporation or the Union. The demand shall state in detail the nature of the complaint . . .

It will be noted that the Adjustment Board (a form of permanent arbitration) is given jurisdiction over matters directly related to provisions of the agreement, whereas ad hoc arbitration is agreed to for all matters not covered by the contract but arising during its term.

In contrast to these examples of broad jurisdiction, the following excerpts from contracts indicate restrictive clauses.

Example No. 1 (medium-size steel company)

The arbitrator shall not have the power to add to, subtract from, alter, or modify in any manner any of the terms of this Agreement, or any agreement supplemental hereto. Any case appealed to the arbitrator on which he determines he has no power to rule shall be referred back to the parties without decision or recommendation . . .

Example No. 2 (medium-size company in automotive industry)

The power of the arbitrator stems from this agreement and his function is to interpret and apply this agreement and any other agreement which the parties may enter into supplemental thereto. He shall have no power to add to, or substract from or modify, any of the terms of this agreement or any of the terms of any agreement which may be supplemental thereto, except as such power may be conferred upon him by any of the provisions of this or any other agreement into which the parties may enter.

Example No. 3 (southern textile company)

It is specifically agreed, however, that such Impartial Umpire must base his decision on the facts as ascertained and determined by him and terms of this contract. He shall have no power to render a decision the effect of which is to change or modify any provision of the contract or write into it any provision not agreed on by the parties.

Another interesting example of a restrictive contract is one in the chemical industry which first itemizes six types of issues which are within the arbitrator's jurisdiction, and then four types of issues which are not subject to arbitration, and concludes with the following general provision:

The Arbitration Panel shall not have the power to amend or supplement the provisions of this Agreement . . .

These examples and many others similar to them show that virtually all agreements give the arbitrator jurisdiction over:

1. Issues involving alleged violations of the agreement.
2. Questions directly involving interpretation and application of provisions of the agreement.

The borderline between restrictive and broad jurisdiction depends primarily on the handling of the following types of issues:

1. Issues involving or alleged to involve adding to or supplementing the contract.
2. Issues not covered by the contract.

Since this matter of adding to or supplementing the agreement is also a problem in connection with subject matters clearly within the arbitrator's jurisdiction, discussion of its significance will be deferred until later.

Before leaving this phase of the jurisdiction question, it is important to note that the foregoing analysis was based on language of the agreements studied. Language of the agreement may not tell the whole story as respects the real position and practice of the parties. I have arbitrated cases in contracts giving me relatively broad jurisdiction by agreement language where it is apparent that one or both parties have a general concept of limited jurisdiction. Conversely, there are instances where jurisdiction by contract language is limited, but the actual practice is different. I am not known as an arbitrator who is partial to limited jurisdiction. However, a surprisingly large number of cases have been presented to me for decision on the merits which would not be arbitrable by strict application of the arbitration clause. In a number of such cases I have called the attention of the parties to the jurisdiction problem at the hearing, even though they have not mentioned it. The somewhat shamefaced response can frequently be paraphrased as follows:

> Yes, we know that this issue is not arbitrable under the terms of our agreement. But it's a real problem to us and we want a solution. We had hoped that nobody would notice the jurisdiction angle.

This sort of situation raises an interesting question. Is the failure of either party to raise a question of jurisdiction in connection with an issue not arbitrable under the contract arbitration language relating to jurisdiction, tantamount to a special stipulation to arbitrate? The answer to that question is probably in the affirmative. However, a deeper problem is whether the same parties will adopt the same attitude in the next roughly comparable situation. If attitudes are consistent there is no serious problem, and the parties will eventually see to it that their contract language catches up with their practices. But if attitudes of the parties are not likely to be consistent, the arbitrator may be well advised to raise the jurisdiction question and secure the equivalent of a special stipulation in that case. In any event, the parties should be aware of the possible conflict between the terms of their agreement defining the arbitrator's authority and the nature of the issue being presented to arbitration.

Latitude in Decision-making within Subject Matters over Which the Arbitrator Does Have Jurisdiction.

If the arbitrator does have jurisdiction over the subject matter of a dispute, the next question is the latitude given to him by the parties or desired by them in disposing of the issue.

Specific Limitations

Some agreements contain specific limitations in this area. For example, there is the occasional contract which provides in the case of discharge that the arbitrator is limited to a finding of guilt or innocence of the offense charged. No latitude is given in the matter of back pay. If "guilty as charged" the discharge stands. If "not guilty as charged" the employee must be reinstated with full back pay. The arbitrator is not permitted any discretion to determine whether the punishment fits the crime. The opposite of such limitations is suggested by the following clause:

> In the case of a discharged employee, if the facts developed during the investigation justify the reinstatement of the aggrieved employee, the Arbitrator shall determine the amount of back pay due the employee, if any.

Many agreements also contain specific limitations or instructions in the matter of retroactivity. The following clause is illustrative:

> Awards or settlements of grievances shall in no case be made retroactive beyond the date on which the grievance was first

presented in written form in Step 2 above, except as provided in Articles III and XII of this Agreement.

As is the case with specific limitations on subject matter, specific limitations of action in disposing of an issue do not often present major problems to the arbitrator even though some of them may become undesirable to the parties.

Factors Which the Arbitrator May Consider

The principal problems in this general area arise out of differences in basic concepts as to the types of evidence and testimony which an arbitrator should consider in making his award, and the relative weights to be given to these various factors. It is seldom that a contract is specific on these vital matters. Types of evidence and testimony often presented to arbitrators include:

1. The contract language.
2. Intent of the parties.
3. Past practice.
4. Practice at other plants in the same industry or in other industries.
5. Equity.
6. Arbitration precedents.
7. Good industrial relations practices.

Regardless of the extent of jurisdiction conferred on the arbitrator, contract language pertinent to the issue is usually called to the attention of the arbitrator and is vital to the decision in the case. No arbitrator in his right mind wants to change the clear-cut terms of an agreement, whatever may be his personal views on the subject matter. However, virtually all grievances and complaints for which there is a clear answer in the agreement are disposed of at an early stage of the grievance procedure and never reach arbitration. Out of some two thousand arbitration decisions issued by the writer over a period of twelve years, not more than five per cent of the cases were issues concerning which the contract provided a clear and unmistakable answer. These are the easy cases when they do arise. The difficulty with the original umpire concept, discussed earlier, is that it applies directly to such a small proportion of cases.

The next type of evidence and testimony concerns the intent of the parties. Oral testimony concerning discussions at the time the negotiators wrote the pertinent language, background of plant situations out of which the language developed, written notes kept by the parties or transcripts of negotiating sessions—all these factors may shed light on the real intent of the parties. Even at this level, fundamental differences in basic concepts begin to emerge. Some parties would have the arbitrator look only at the written words and object to any consideration of intent. Others stress intent and tend to belittle the language. Here again, it is not uncommon for parties to be inconsistent, varying their position according to the case at hand.

Past practice of the parties themselves in applying the disputed contract language is often introduced as the best evidence of intent. The really difficult cases are the not infrequent situations where demonstrated and fairly consistent past practice over an appreciable period of time has been at variance with the contract language.

Testimony and evidence concerning practice at other plants in the same industry, in the same area, or even in other industries outside the area are often introduced. While this type of evidence is one or more steps removed from the plant involved in the dispute, it is well known that occasions arise where this factor is of some importance.

One of the most debatable questions concerns the weight which should be given to general considerations of equity. Positions of various parties fluctuate all the way from those who believe that equity should not be a factor in grievance arbitration to those who hold that it should be a major consideration in virtually all cases.

Since the Bureau of National Affairs, Prentice-Hall, Inc., and other organizations have published arbitration awards in recent years, arbitrators have been confronted with decisions issued by fellow arbitrators in situations alleged to be comparable to the case at hand. For an even longer period it has been common for the parties to introduce in evidence arbitration decisions issued earlier at the same plant or in the same industry. In the permanent arbitration arrangements, most parties give great weight to earlier awards under the same contract. Where ad hoc arbitration is the system adopted by the parties there is a tendency for them to try their luck on the same issue again with a different arbitrator. The parties and arbitrators generally agree that the weight to be given to other awards diminishes as the locale of these other awards moves away from the plant or industry involved.

In addition to general considerations of equity, some parties and some arbitrators tend to place considerable weight on so-called good industrial relations practices. As a general proposition, I believe that most companies and unions are not very receptive to this approach, and for sound reasons. What may be good for any two parties at a given time and place is primarily dependent on their own thinking and stage of development. Moreover, there are few subject matters in grievance arbitration in which anyone can afford to be very dogmatic in distinguishing the good from the not good. These observations do not exclude the possibility of suggestions based on experience of others. What is distasteful is the foisting of preconceived ideas on unwilling recipients.

The foregoing brief résumé of types of evidence and testimony may be even more relevant to the general question of jurisdiction of the arbitrator than the more formal and usual discussion of specific or general contractual limitations on the arbitrator's authority. Since only a very small percentage of cases can be answered directly out of the contract language, the disposition of the bulk of the cases is dependent on the concepts held by the parties and by the arbitrator as to how these other types of evidence and testimony are to be utilized in any given set of circumstances.

No general answers can be devised which would fix the relative weight to be given to each type of evidence. However, there is one generalization which the writer believes to be valid. In the earlier steps of the grievance procedure, most parties develop mores or ways of thinking which give some indication of the relative weight which they give to these various factors in the vast majority of grievances settled without outside intervention. *It is the considered judgment of the writer that arbitration decisions are most acceptable when they fit just as closely as possible into the pattern and method of thinking which the parties utilize in their own settlements of grievances.* If arbitration awards depart too far from these patterns they may be quite unacceptable, and arbitration has not fulfilled its essential function as a substitute for the use of economic force. This is one of the reasons why the trend is toward permanent arbitration arrangements. The arbitrator is better able to appreciate and discern the basic attitudes of the parties in these respects than is possible in ad hoc systems. There remains one fundamental difference between the practices of the parties and sound practice for the arbitrator. The parties are free to change their agreement at any time. The arbitrator is not empowered to do so.

Management Prerogative

Underlying the distinction between liberal and restrictive contract provisions or practices respecting jurisdiction of the arbitrator are varying concepts of management prerogative. One point of view held by some management representatives is the idea that all areas of industrial relations consist of rights retained exclusively by the company until and unless the union carves out some segment or segments of these rights and limits them by specific written agreement provisions. This concept is illustrated by an agreement clause which reads:

> Except as otherwise in this Agreement expressly provided, nothing in this Agreement contained shall be deemed to limit the Company in any way in the exercise of the regular and customary functions of management.

In this same contract the grievance procedure is all-inclusive. It begins with the words:

Any matter which in the opinion of the Union or any Employee requires adjustment . . .

However, when the grievance procedure comes to the arbitration step, arbitration is limited by the words:

. . . if any such grievance shall involve the interpretation or application of the provisions of this Agreement . . .

Unlimited grievance procedure but limited arbitration is consistent with this management-prerogative clause and with the basic concept illustrated. The company is free to make an agreement with the union at any time prior to arbitration which carves out still another segment from the large body of management rights, but the arbitrator is not empowered to do so.

The opposite of this concept may be discerned in the extensive jurisdiction clauses reproduced earlier in this chapter or in the following additional illustration:

. . . in the event differences should arise between the Company and the Union or its members employed by the Company as to the meaning and application of this agreement, or should any trouble of any kind arise in the plant . . .

These differences in concept of management prerogative go much deeper than jurisdiction of the arbitrator. They lie at the heart of the parties' ideas of the scope of collective bargaining. Arbitrators work in these different environments, and it would be unrealistic and presumptuous for any arbitrator to assume that he could function in the same manner under the two agreements used in the above illustrations.

It may be partly extraneous to this paper to comment on trends of thinking about management prerogative. However, it is not an opinion or a value judgment, but is a fact that the exponents of the extreme concept of management prerogative have been fighting a losing battle. Whether under the carving-away hypothesis or by voluntary grant of management, the scope of collective bargaining has been expanding steadily. In a few situations the expansion may have moved too far. The essential management prerogative is the right to initiate. The necessity of subjecting management decisions in the area of labor relations to an arbitrator for scrutiny and possible reversal may be objectionable to many company representatives. But it is a small price to pay if it is compared with a possible alternative, the loss of the right to initiate.

The "May Not Add to or Supplement" Limitation

The "may not add to or supplement" limitation on the arbitrator's jurisdiction causes, or should cause, much soul searching on the part of arbitrators and the parties. The general background of the clause has been explored in earlier parts of this chapter. An attempt will be made here to indicate the practical problems in applying the clause.

At the outset, I venture the opinion that many arbitration decisions issued under contracts containing the "may not add to or supplement" prohibition really do add to or supplement the contract. Nor is this situation due in large measure to lack of awareness of the problem by arbitrators. The parties themselves are involved in the conspiracy. The basic reason is that the words "may not add to or supplement" are inadequate and to a substantial degree inaccurate. Even the relatively infrequent open-and-shut case, decided solely on clear and unmistakable contract language, adds to the contract in one respect. It is a reaffirmation of a contract provision adding weight to the original language.

Just as soon as we depart from the open-and-shut case and get into the real field for arbitration the "may not add to or supplement" prohibition becomes unrealistic. If the contract clause is ambiguous, or if there is a conflict between two clauses as applied to a particular set of circumstances, or if past practice deviates from the written word, what arbitrator or what parties can say that nothing has been added to the contract by any decision which may be issued? That is the purpose of taking the matter to arbitration. Moreover, that is what the parties are doing all the time in their own settlement of grievances. They are giving more meaning to the bare language. It is inevitable that arbitration, the terminal step of the grievance procedure, will accomplish the same result.

Yet the "may not add to or supplement" clause does have meaning despite its inadequacy. What the parties are trying to say is that they do not want an arbitrator to usurp their essential function of collective bargaining. They are willing to let him function on the fringes of collective bargaining but not in the main pasture. In view of the inadequacy of the distinction, the losing party in a case is understandably inclined to criticize the arbitrator for allegedly stepping over the border. The winning party welcomes the fact that the arbitrator accepted jurisdiction or even supports an indiscretion. But on the very next case the reactions may be reversed. The arbitrator's problem is that it is extremely difficult for him to discern where the borderline is, quite apart from the differing positions of the parties on this score. It is only in the permanent arbitration arrangements that the arbitrator can gradually obtain a feel for the real positions of the parties in this matter apart from their positions in specific cases. There is a real need in agreement-writing for a satisfactory substitute for the words "may not add to or supplement."

Issues Not Covered by the Contract

Somewhat clearer jurisdiction distinctions exist with respect to the not infrequent disputes on which the contract language is silent. Some parties meet this type of jurisdiction problem squarely by granting authority to the arbitrator in unmistakable language, such as:

> In the event any differences or disputes arise between the parties as to the meaning, application or interpretation of any of the terms or conditions of this agreement that cannot be amicably settled, or should either party claim that the other has breached any of the terms or conditions of this agreement, *or should any grievance or dispute remain unsettled* after exhausting the first three steps of the grievance procedure outlined in Article XXV hereof, then, the dispute or question involved, except those specifically excluded in this agreement, shall be submitted for arbitration, to an arbitrator to be mutually selected by the parties, as herein provided. (Italics supplied)

Others are just as forthright in the opposite direction in their contract language. An issue not covered by the contract is usually encompassed within the "may not add to or supplement" limitation just discussed. However, denial of jurisdiction to the arbitrator in such matters sometimes leads to strange results.

There is a fairly sizable number of cases submitted to arbitration where the grievance or complaint does not meet the issue because of the jurisdiction problem. The patient has a stomachache, and everybody except the arbitrator knows that it is a variety of stomachache. There is nothing in the contract about stomachaches, but there is a clause about ingrowing toenails. The grievance is presented to the arbitrator as a violation of the ingrowing-toenail clause in the hope that the patient will be distracted long enough for the stomachache to correct itself, or in the hope that the arbitrator's prescription for the toenail will somehow fix the stomach disorder, or in the hope that the arbitrator will discern the true malady and prescribe for it. These tactics of obfuscation under contracts granting no jurisdiction where the contract is silent sometimes work. But if they do work it is because the patient is so healthy that he is stronger than the medicine. If he is not that healthy, he erupts and makes a mess of things generally during elaborate scrutiny of the toenail. This is a crude and extreme analogy, but the facts of life in some of these cases are not much different. An actual situation will be reviewed briefly.

A company presented a complaint to the arbitrator asking him to issue a decision providing that the company has the right to conduct time studies. At the outset of the hearing there was some shadow boxing around the question whether the word "studies" in the labor agreement included time studies. It soon became apparent that there was no possible doubt on that score. The company would be supported completely on the issue submitted. But it also became apparent that the issuance of that decision would be of no appreciable value to anybody. The real problem was that earlier time studies had been badly mismanaged. Employee resentment had developed to such an emotional pitch that a short work stoppage had occurred already, and few employees could think rationally about any phase of time study. The only realistic approach to that major problem was to decide the limited issue submitted and then discuss the real problem. The parties began to confess their respective errors at a continuation of the hearing, which was conducted as an informal conference. From that beginning they started to build a sound basis by which employee objections to time study would not arise again.

Relationship Between Jurisdiction and Acceptability

All the various phases of the jurisdiction problem which have just been discussed are related quite directly to the fundamental concept that grievance arbitration is the contractual trade for the no-strike, no-lockout clause. With full recognition of the soundness of the motives which impel some parties to agree to restrictive arbitration clauses, the dilemma created in such cases is that the trade is incomplete if the arbitrator is restricted too severely.

Some parties recognize this fact. An illustration is the following clause from an agreement:

> The Employer recognizes the right of the Local Union to strike on any issue not subject to the jurisdiction of the Impartial Umpire . . .

However, probably a majority of contracts do not recognize the dilemma. The no-strike, no-lockout clause is all inclusive, but at the same time there may be severe limitations, both specific and general, on the authority of the arbitrator. This sort of agreement can be a very valid agreement if both parties understand its nature. A trade does not have to be complete to make it a bargain. A union can even agree not to strike for a year's time if no arbitration of any sort is provided.

The acceptability problem arises because the true nature of the incomplete bargain is often not understood by union officials and even less by employees. The acceptability of an arbitration award denying jurisdiction over an issue is not enhanced when the implications of the incomplete bargain sneak up on one of the parties. Any appreciable number of such decisions can destroy the system. In short, the entire discussion of jurisdiction in this paper is in the nature of an appeal to companies and unions generally to think through the implications of their arbitration clause. Any agreement reached, whether in the direction of extensive jurisdiction or toward limited jurisdiction, can be satisfactory so long as both parties understand it.

METHODS AND PROCEDURAL TECHNIQUES WHICH ARBITRATORS MAY UTILIZE TO INCREASE ACCEPTABILITY OF THE PROCESS

The purpose of this chapter is to attempt to indicate some of the methods and techniques which arbitrators may utilize in seeking to improve the acceptability of the arbitration process and of awards. This attempt is necessarily accompanied by liberal doses of humility and qualifications. If an arbitrator is fortunate enough to really develop an acceptable solution in a case, it may be difficult for him to determine how it was done. Moreover, the same methods will not work satisfactorily for other issues or for the same issue with other parties. However, some methods and techniques may have enough general significance to warrant the exploration.

Types of Cases Submitted to Arbitration

Exploration of methods and techniques begins with an examination of types of cases commonly submitted to arbitration. Largely irrespective of subject matter, grievance-arbitration cases can be divided into five general types.

The first type is relatively infrequent, but of major importance. It is the genuine difference of opinion which is so critical that a strike or lockout would probably develop over the issue if arbitration were not available as an alternative.

Or a strike has already occurred and has been terminated by an agreement to arbitrate. The situation is encumbered by a high degree of emotional tension.

The next type is no less genuine as a legitimate dispute. The essential difference is that, by itself, the issue probably is not one which would result directly in a strike or a lockout. Nevertheless the parties have been unable to reach agreement after reasonable attempts to do so. If not arbitrated, the unresolved issue and others like it would remain as sore points which might unduly complicate the next contract negotiations, or even contribute to a strike or lockout at that time. Or a series of such unresolved matters may build up to an explosive situation which could be touched off by almost any kind of spark.

The third type of issue is one which goes to arbitration only because the earlier steps of the grievance procedure have been inadequate. Real possibilities of settlement have always existed, but for one reason or another the grievance procedure has not been a suitable medium for development of the answer.

The fourth type is the face-saving case. Persons on both sides of the table have a joint answer, but it is advisable or expedient to have an arbitrator take the rap. A union election may be in the offing, and one or more representatives think that they cannot afford to take an unpopular position. The personnel manager for the company may not have the authority to decide the case, and has been unable to persuade his superiors. A union official may believe that a shop steward has become too officious and needs a public defeat. Or a foreman cannot be handled adequately by top supervision and needs a spanking. These face-saving cases are no small part of the total arbitration case load.

A fifth type is the throw-in case. It is a sad commentary on arbitration that many parties feel that to insure a favorable decision in a really good case, it is advisable to throw in one or more losing cases as offsets. This is not just a union practice. Some companies, facing known arbitration of a legitimate dispute, resort to the same tactics and see to it that one or more cases which the union is likely to win will be included at the hearings before the same arbitrator.

It is obvious that the sound basis for grievance arbitration is the existence of the first two types of cases. The last three types are illegitimate by purely objective standards. However, these types of cases are part of the facts of life in many relationships, and the arbitrator is naïve who is unaware of their existence. If the practice is not abused, the third and fourth types have occasional real value. The fifth type is scarcely defensible on any basis.

It should be quite obvious that the methods and procedures adopted by the arbitrator will necessarily vary, depending on the type of case presented to him. The first type of case may be so critical that the arbitrator's behavior, as well as his award, may make the difference between a peaceful solution and a question as to advisability of continuing the system of arbitration. The second type of case is less important as a single case, but the overall appraisal by the parties of a series of such cases may have the same result. In the third type of case the arbitrator has the responsibility to help put collective bargaining back on the track to avoid excessive and unnecessary use of the procedure. In the face-saving type of case the arbitrator needs to be aware of the dangers of overuse of the device. And in those face-saving cases which the arbitrator must decide, no greater error can be committed than to issue an award that nobody wants. Arbitrators are the only ones who can demonstrate by their actions that the throw-in case is a mistake and seldom achieves any useful result.

Methods

There is some overlap between methods and procedural techniques as they will be discussed hereafter. However, the term "methods" is intended to relate to the arbitrator's approach to a case at the hearing largely irrespective of the type of arbitration in effect.

Obtaining Understanding of the Position of Each Party

One of the principal functions of the oral hearing is to enable the arbitrator to obtain an understanding of the position of each party. It should be obvious that no decision in a case can be acceptable unless the arbitrator knows what he is deciding. This need goes beyond the mere acquisition of sufficient knowledge of the facts of the case and comparison of the facts with the pertinent contract clauses. In so far as possible the arbitrator needs to know some of the more intangible reasons for the position of the parties. In some respects the arbitrator needs to be a triple personality. He should be able to secure a sympathetic understanding of all the reasons why the union is taking the position it does take. Similarly, he should be able to put himself in the shoes of the company representatives to obtain a sympathetic understanding of that position. In this connection it may be helpful for the arbitrator to summarize the position of each party at the hearing as he understands it, to make certain that he has obtained the full position. An even more important purpose of such summaries is to enable the representatives of each side of the argument to conclude that the arbitrator begins his deliberations in the presence of all the necessary background. It is a common criticism of arbitrators that they not only issued a wrong decision, but that they did not even understand the problem. I have even heard criticism from the winning side in a case on the contention that though the decision was right it was based on a far from complete understanding of the issue. In short, a first requisite to acceptability is understanding. To use a common expression, a decision is much more palatable if both sides have a feeling that the arbitrator knows what it's all about.

The third aspect of the triple personality idea comes into the picture because there is a danger that either or both parties may obtain the impression that the arbitrator is unduly sympathetic with the position of one of the parties. Reasonable care in summarizing positions is necessary. *Sympathetic understanding is not the same thing as identifica-*

tion. The arbitrator's impartial position must be preserved, not only in his own thinking, but in the parties' appraisal of his attitude.

Defining the Issue

After the initial or opening statements of both parties it is often necessary to define the issues. In grievance arbitration the stipulation is usually the original written grievance. This may be poorly worded. Or the discussion at earlier steps of the grievance procedure may have developed the issue in different or modified channels. Because the parties have lived with the case through earlier grievance meetings, they may assume that the arbitrator knows more about the case than he can possibly know. It is not infrequent that some time is required before the issue can be discerned clearly. In an occasional case, the parties themselves may be surprised when they finally find out just what the issue is. This process of defining the issue can cut away much of the surplus baggage that accumulates around many grievances. In some instances, defining the issue is all that may be needed to secure a settlement of the problem.

Determining Extent of Agreement

Another useful step is to determine the extent of agreement on factual background and applicable contract terms. In some cases the parties agree on all the pertinent facts and on the applicable contract provisions. Full attention can then be directed to argument and evidence as to how the contract terms should be applied to the agreed-upon facts. At the opposite extreme, there are cases where there appears at the outset to be no agreement on anything. For example, I have heard discharge cases where the only initial agreement was on the identity of the discharged employee and the approximate date of the discharge. Even in such cases, painstaking efforts at the hearing will usually develop a surprising amount of agreement on many important aspects of the case. On some aspects of the case where disagreement persists, the parties may be able to agree that these are inconsequential phases of the case anyway. In short, this is a narrowing-down process which enables the parties and the arbitrator to direct their major attention to the important disputed elements.

Clarifying and Delimiting the Disputed Aspects of the Case

Even within the disputed elements of the case, the same essential process of narrowing down can be continued. To illustrate again by a discharge case, a reasonably clear picture may gradually emerge of what happened at the time of the incident. The "crime" may become established with sufficient accuracy to make additional pursuit of the details relatively meaningless. But the parties are still in complete disagreement on the fundamental question whether the punishment fits the crime. From that point on, testimony and evidence can be concentrated on the patterns developed by the parties themselves in earlier cases. What has become acceptable as reasonable discipline or just cause in earlier cases? What is the employee's seniority, and what weight, if any, have the parties given to this factor in earlier cases? Is there a general pattern of warnings, suspensions, etc., before the final act of discharge in some types of cases? If so, is the present case that general type of case, and what is the employee's past record? Such explorations can sometimes lead to agreement. If agreement is not possible, the decision is more likely to be acceptable.

Raising Doubts

It is not uncommon that the two parties come into a hearing with different sets of facts, presumably directed to the same point. Sometimes these factual statements are honestly presented but turn out to be inaccurate because they are based on incomplete information. Or the differences in the facts may be due to different periods of time over which they have been computed or differences in the sample selected. Questions directed by each party to the other, or questions raised by the arbitrator based on experience in analyzing factual data, can frequently result in basic agreement on these facts. Or if no agreement is achieved it is at least possible to ascertain a reasonably complete background of each separate set of facts, a process which is essential before they can be appraised properly. If one or both of the parties have predicated their positions on their own honest concept of the facts, and more complete investigation discloses doubts about this basic background, a foundation may have been established for an agreement or for a more acceptable award.

The same process of deflation can take place by full exploration of the relative importance of the various arguments. It is very understandable that both parties will often seize upon one or more arguments which support their position. It is easy to magnify these elements of the case honestly, and to turn the telescope the other way around when looking at other phases of the same case. The hearing can serve the function of raising doubts in the minds of one or both parties as to the real magnitude of their strong points. It can take off the glasses on both sides of the table.

Another method of raising doubts in the minds of one or both parties is to raise a question as to the implication of their present position under different assumed circumstances, or in the light of different but related problems known to exist. It might be assumed that the parties themselves would have examined these implications already. However, it is understandable that there are situations where fully competent representatives of the parties have lived so close to a situation that they can't see the forest for the trees. An arbitrator sometimes has an advantage because he does come into the case cold. He may be in a better position to view the scene in better perspective. An extreme example of this idea may be summarized briefly. A company and a union came into a hearing and argued furiously for approximately an hour about an overtime-pay question. The principal arguments were predicated on a recent unsigned and incomplete agreement. With knowledge of the background of this situation the arbitrator asked one simple question. There was a startled hush in the room. It was almost possible to see the wheels grind to a stop and then reverse. From that point on, both sides changed places and argued with equal vigor in opposition to their original positions. What had happened was that both parties had lost sight of a larger issue in their enthusiasm about a relatively minor one.

These various aspects of the method of raising doubts at a hearing can sometimes lead to settlement of the issue by the parties. If that is not possible a decision is more likely to be acceptable. Here again, the permanent arbitrator is in a much better position to utilize this method than an ad hoc arbitrator.

Relationship between Methods and Type of Case

No blueprint can be drawn to show just how and when the methods indicated above can or should be used. The arbitrator can only do his best to obtain a feel of the case and act accordingly. He must play it by ear. Moreover, ability to sense when one or more of these methods should not be used may be just as important or even more important than when they should be used. For example, overuse of some of these methods in a face-saving type of case could be most embarrassing and almost disastrous.

The methods discussed above can be used by the arbitrator in varying degree under any system of arbitration or even under most concepts of the arbitrator's function. There may be a few instances of the extreme of legalistic presentation where one or both parties may object to the raising-doubts idea, but these are the exceptional cases. The more basic consideration is that the arbitrator must be extremely careful not to dominate the proceeding. His most important job is to listen, not to talk. Most arbitrators need to fight off a tendency to play god. The timing of the questions he may want to ask, or the direction of discussion he may want to suggest, is of the utmost importance. As a general proposition, the arbitrator should not inject himself into the discussion until after the initial presentations or until after the parties themselves have begun to run out of gas.

In concluding this section on methods an analogy may not

be inappropriate. The Quakers are a small religious group who have a theory about conducting business meetings. The basic feature of this theory is that it is possible to reconcile all differences by conscientious and painstaking exchange of views. Votes are never taken, and majority rule is not the practice. The theory is that final action should be taken only after the group is united in that action. The clerk of the meeting presides. When he believes that unity has been achieved he enters a record of the action. The expression used is: "It is the sense of the meeting that . . ." As is true of all theories, Quaker practice is not always consistent with belief. There are numerous known instances of railroading or insensitive disregard for minority opinion. However, there is a basic validity to the idea which is transferable to the present subject matter. It is sometimes possible for the arbitrator to be clerk of the meeting and so conduct the proceedings that basic unity is obtained out of free discussion of a common problem. To the extent that the arbitrator can act as a catalytic agent in this process, acceptability of the system and of awards is enhanced.

Procedural Techniques

In some contrast to the methods just discussed, use or non-use of the following procedural techniques will necessarily vary appreciably, depending on the type of arbitration system in effect, the concepts of the parties about the function of arbitration, and the type of case. With these qualifications in mind there may be some value in indicating some of these techniques.

Settlement of a Case by the Parties at the Hearing

It is not infrequent that discussion at a hearing develops a basis for settlement of the issue by the parties. If that happens the purposes of the grievance procedure have been fulfilled. The newly adopted Code of Ethics and Procedural Standards for Labor-Management Arbitration developed by the American Arbitration Association and the National Academy of Arbitrators treats this subject as follows:

> He [the arbitrator] should not undertake to induce a settlement of the dispute against the wishes of either party. If, however, an atmosphere is created or the issues are so simplified or reduced as to lead to a voluntary settlement of the parties, a function of of his office has been fulfilled.

Settlement by the parties may take a variety of forms, of which three may be noted briefly.

If the moving party finds that it does not have a good case, the complaint may be withdrawn. Withdrawal of a complaint under such circumstances has a number of advantages. The cost of the proceeding will be reduced because the arbitrator will not have to write an opinion. Withdrawal of a case may create an atmosphere of good will in which the other party may settle other pending grievances. Moreover, a case withdrawn is ordinarily preferred by the losing party to a formal adverse award.

In the opposite sort of situation the discussion may indicate that the complaint is justified. The defending party, coming to the realization that it does not have a good defense, may want to grant the request for the same reasons noted in the preceding paragraph.

These two types of settlement are emphasized because there is a common impression that settlement means compromise. Discussion of the best sort at a hearing often means the development of a willingness to lose.

The third type of settlement is the compromise settlement. The word "compromise" may be used in a variety of ways. It may mean a settlement which neither side wants or likes, but is adopted solely as a not too unpalatable answer to dispose of the case and to enable the parties to get on to other business. Such settlements may be fairly common at earlier steps of the grievance procedure, but are not often effectuated after a case goes as far as an arbitration hearing. They sometimes come about at hearings if both parties become so fearful of what the arbitrator may do that they prefer to choose a known lesser evil rather than take a chance on a potentially greater one. The better type of compromise settlement arises when constructive discussion at the hearing discloses that the facts of the situation require an in-between answer.

Hearing Recess for Purposes of Direct Negotiation

If the relationship between the arbitrator and the parties and between the parties themselves is informal, settlements of any of the three types indicated above may be reached around the hearing table in the presence of all participants. However, in other situations or under some circumstances even in an informal atmosphere, it is often advisable for the arbitrator to recess the hearing to enable the parties to caucus among their own representatives or to conduct direct negotiations in the absence of the arbitrator. At the conclusion of the recess the parties report to the arbitrator the fact that a settlement has been achieved or, if the direct negotiation has not been successful, the hearing proceeds.

The suggestion of a recess often comes from one of the parties. If it does not, and the arbitrator feels that a recess might be fruitful, he may make the suggestion. The reactions to the suggestion will ordinarily indicate whether the arbitrator has been correct in his appraisal. A recess for direct negotiation should not be forced on unwilling parties.

Requests for Additional Information

It was noted earlier that the determination of the extent of agreement and the narrowing-down process in a case often discloses differences of opinion about facts, which differences may be ironed out by more complete investigation. Another fairly common development is that the discussion at the hearing may indicate the need for additional factual material which cannot be obtained on short notice. If the information noted above is important to the case, the parties or the arbitrator may indicate the type of information needed, and a timetable may be determined for securing the data.

There are two general methods of procedure when this situation arises. One is that the necessary information will be secured by one or both parties and presented at an adjourned hearing. However, to avoid the expense involved in such a procedure it is often possible to obtain agreement on presentation of such additional information in the form of briefs or letters submitted to the arbitrator and exchanged between the parties. In some circumstances the parties will agree to secure the information jointly, or to have it initialed by representatives of both sides. If the information obtained is not agreed upon, opportunity is given for comments by both parties. If the additional information is quite controversial, a continued hearing may be necessary.

Referral Back to the Parties

Where settlement of a case is not obtained at the hearing, but there are real indications that further direct negotiations may be desirable, the hearing may be concluded with the understanding that the parties will meet for further discussion after the hearing and will report to the arbitrator within a specific period of time. In such situations a decision is issued only if the report indicates negative results of the direct negotiation.

In cases where additional information is to be submitted and is important to the case, the parties will usually want to make another attempt to settle the matter in the light of all the facts.

This in another area in which the arbitrator must exercise his best judgment by appraisal of the reactions of the parties. If there is no real likelihood that settlement will be achieved, referral of the case back to the parties can simply be time-consuming and irritating. In some face-saving cases the insistence of the arbitrator on this procedure could be doubly irritating. But if the parties are abusing the face-saving device by over-use or by attempting to perpetrate an improper deal, there may be situations where the arbitrator may properly object to becoming a tool of the parties. The essential consideration is that an agreement of the parties is better than a decision, and all reasonable efforts to assist such agreement are valid.

Mediation

The ideas suggested in an earlier section (methods which may be utilized by the arbitrator at the hearing) are in reality forms of mediation. To the extent that the arbitrator may be able to assist the parties at the hearing to define or clarify the issues, narrow down or delimit the differences in points of view, or secure a more complete and unbiased appraisal of their own positions, he has acted as a mediator as well as an arbitrator. If the result is a settlement of the case without issuance of a decision, it is in essence a mediated solution.

There is a sharp difference of opinion among companies, unions and arbitrators as to whether mediation efforts should extend beyond the methods and procedural techniques already discussed.

There is, however, one additional area in which forms of mediation are generally accepted. The tripartite arbitration board, an arbitration system already discussed, is usually designed and intended as a device for mediation efforts beyond those possible at a hearing. The methods which may be employed by the arbitrator are basically the same that he may use at a hearing. The essential difference is that the executive sessions of an arbitration board are less formal, the participants are few in number, and the sessions are semi-confidential in nature. If the tripartite board functions as intended, and the arbitrator and the party representatives coöperate in the process, a mediated settlement is much more likely to become a reality. This may be true even in those cases where there is a dissent for the record. In short, the tripartite board carries the hearing process one step further.

The sharp differences of opinion exist about one additional possible step. It is well known that there a few arbitration systems, characterized by the true form of the impartial chairman concept, where both parties expect and even insist that the arbitrator meet with the parties, jointly or separately or both, after the hearing for discussion of the issues and of the prospective decision. Except for the fact that this system is informal rather than formal, there is only one usual difference between it and a tripartite board. Under most tripartite board arrangements the discussion is in executive session with all representatives present. Under some impartial chairman systems it is clearly understood that the arbitrator may meet with the parties separately.

Probably a majority of companies and unions oppose this form of mediation unless it is formalized by the establishment of a tripartite board. The principal objection is to the discussion of the issues, and particularly of a proposed decision, with one or more representatives of one of the parties in the absence of the other party representatives. The objections are based on a number of fears. One is that the arbitrator is likely to be influenced most by the last person consulted. Another is that alleged evidence pertinent to the case may be transmitted which will influence the arbitrator and which the other party has no effective opportunity to challenge. Another is that the arbitrator will make deals to enhance his popularity, or that commitments made separately with one party cannot then be altered, even if the arbitrator finds that the commitment was based on incomplete or inaccurate information. Another less likely but occasional fear is that one of the parties will directly or indirectly bribe the arbitrator.

All these fears are possible realities. After some experience under such systems, I should be the last person to say that there is no danger to the parties and to the arbitrator. The essential question is whether the benefits are worth the risks involved. On this score, the best evidence is that few companies and unions who have developed the impartial chairman concept have abandoned it, and that there is a discernible tendency toward more extensive use of the system, at least up to the point of separate discussions with party representatives, which is the most common stopping point.

What are the benefits of the impartial chairman concept? The basic advantage is that acceptable decisions are much more likely to be issued. Matters submitted to arbitration can be so complex that the possibility of trying on a decision for size is of immeasurable assistance to the arbitrator, and avoids unworkable or unsound decisions. Even in the area of opinion-writing an arbitrator can issue a decision which is fully acceptable, but he can write something in the opinion which, unknown to him, can stir up more trouble than the original dispute. If a responsible representative of each party can read the entire decision and opinion before it has been issued, such unfortunate results can be eliminated. Advance discussion with a representative of the losing party can often serve to soften the blow of an adverse decision by more adequate explanation than is possible in the written word delivered by mail.

While it is the personal opinion of the writer that the impartial chairman concept is superior to the more generally accepted methods of arbitration, I am even more thoroughly convinced that that system should not be foisted on any company or union unless it is understood and desired. As has been emphasized throughout this paper, the essential point in most disputable areas of arbitration is the necessity of reasonable agreement and understanding by the parties themselves of their own system and its adaptability to their own needs.

Decision on One Phase of a Case and Referral Back to the Parties of Remaining Issues

Leaving the question of mediation, and returning to most types of cases under most systems, there is another procedural technique which is frequently desirable. Grievances often encompass a number of separable issues or separable phases of the same issue. The case, as presented, shows clearly that there is one point (major or sometimes minor) on which the parties cannot agree, but once over the hump on that point there is every reason to believe that all other matters could be resolved by the parties themselves.

Typical illustrations can be found in cases involving incentive pay. One such type of case is the one where the company has reduced a piece rate. It first involves the question whether there has been enough change in the job to justify any change of piece rates. If that question is decided in the affirmative, the collateral issue is the propriety of the newly established rate. If the first question is decided in the negative, the old rate will be reëstablished automatically. Even though the arbitrator may have jurisdiction over both phases of the issue, it may be advisable to decide the first question only, and refer the second back to the parties with a provision that it will be decided later by arbitration if agreement is not reached. This procedure preserves a maximum of direct negotiation, and the arbitrator attempts to stay out of that phase of the case where his competence is most likely to be doubtful. This procedure is not suggested as a universal device. There are many such cases where it is obvious that decision on both questions will be necessary. The first question may be a formality, and the real issue is the level of the new rate. Referral of the real issue back to the parties would be futile.

Another common type of piece-rate case combines a major issue of contract interpretation regarding the proper level of expected earnings, and a minor issue of allowed times as established by a company time study. If the major issue is decided by the arbitrator, there may be a reasonable certainty that the minor issue can be and should be decided by the parties.

In the ad hoc arbitration system, some state laws and court decisions tend to impose limitations on the use of this procedure because of provisions that the arbitrator may not reserve to himself any further jurisdiction of the case after a decision has been issued. The writer does not presume to be a legal authority. However, if a decision of this type is desired by the parties, and this problem is presented or suggested at the hearing, it has been my experience that the problem can be met.

Decision as a Record of Settlement of a Case or as a Record of Tacit Agreement

Even though the parties settle a case at a hearing, there are occasions when they may request the arbitrator to formalize the settlement by a memorandum or even by a full opinion and award. In some instances, the arbitrator is in reality functioning only as a recorder. In others, there may be some element of face-saving in the request. Unless there is some phase of the settlement to which the arbitrator cannot subscribe, most arbitrators have no objection to serving in this capacity if requested to do so.

In other instances, discussion at the hearing may indicate that a particular decision would not be unacceptable to both parties, but for a variety of reasons the decision must be made by the arbitrator. The decision written in these cases is in reality a type of mediated agreement formalized by an award. Again, most arbitrators are entirely willing to perform this function.

Selling the Decision by Means of the Opinion

Companies, unions, and arbitrators have differing ideas about opinion-writing. Some prefer that arbitrators issue only a short memorandum decision, disposing of the issues but giving no reasons. One basis for this position has been noted earlier. It is quite possible for an arbitrator to stir up a hornet's nest by some statement in his opinion which has an adverse effect on the relationship between the parties entirely unpredictable to him when the opinion is written. Another reason is that cost of arbitration may be increased by time required for opinion-writing.

There is still another idea about opinion-writing which is largely discredited. It is the idea that the arbitrator may give one party the opinion and the other the decision. If this idea is ever effectuated it is almost certain to boomerang.

The value of a reasonably well-written opinion extends in several directions. In the first place, it can reassure the parties that the arbitrator understands the case, even if the award itself is not liked. As noted earlier, a primary requisite to acceptability is the belief of the parties that the arbitrator understands the case. Secondly, the parties have been debating the case for some time, and if they desire it they have a right to an appraisal of their arguments. In the third place, if there is validity in the arbitrator's analysis, it can have real educational value and precedent value, if desired, for future cases. Finally, and most important, a well-reasoned opinion can be of value in selling the decision initially to the top representatives on both sides, and finally to employees and supervisors. If the parties and the arbitrator have not laid the necessary groundwork for an acceptable award at the hearing, the written decision and opinion is the last and only opportunity to develop acceptability.

Agreement Preferable to a Decision

The central idea behind many of the procedural techniques which have been outlined above is that an agreement of the parties is almost always preferable to an award. All methods and techniques designed to encourage or facilitate agreement which are consistent with the parties' pattern of collective bargaining in the grievance procedure are valid. Opposition to some of these techniques springs from the conception that no grievance reaches arbitration until after all possible prior steps to reach agreement have been exhausted completely. If this theory should be a fact (as it is consistently in a few collective-bargaining relationships and spasmodically in others), there would be limited opportunity to exercise some of these techniques. Moreover, labored attempts by the arbitrator to induce settlement would be serious mistakes. In this area, again, ability to know when not to make a suggestion may be just as important as the use of the technique at the right time and place. Unfortunately but factually, there is such a sizeable proportion of grievances reaching arbitration where all reasonable attempts to settle the case have not been made, that it has seemed advisable to outline these possible techniques.

In addition to the inadequacies of many grievance procedures there is a much more important consideration. As noted already, the arbitrator always has the possibility of being a catalytic agent in a situation just because he is an outsider and because he can bring a new point of view to the proceedings. He should not overemphasize this position or be too insistent on a settlement. But every settlement which is obtained is a joint achievement of all participants at the hearing. And decisions which come close to a meeting of the minds tend to be more acceptable.

A maxim for arbitration is suggested as follows:

> That decision is best which is not an imposed decision but a meeting of the minds; that decision is next best which embodies a maximum of persuasion and a minimum of command.

www.ingramcontent.com/pod-product-compliance
Lightning Source LLC
LaVergne TN
LVHW011817200926
848484LV00005B/1224